MASTERCLASS

Brazilian Jiu Jitsu

ULTIMATE CHOKING TECHNIQUES

by
Renato Magno

EMPIRE Books
P.O. Box 491788, Los Angeles, CA 90049

Disclaimer

Please note that the author and publisher of this book are NOT RESPONSIBLE in any manner whatsoever for any injury that may result from practicing the techniques and/or following the instructions given within. Since the physical activities described herein may be too strenuous in nature for some readers to engage in safely, it is essential that a physician be consulted prior to training.

Published in 2006 by Empire Books.
Copyright © 2006 by Empire Books.

All rights reserved. No part of this publication may be reproduced or utilized in any form or by any means, electronic or mechanical, including photocopying, recording, or by any information storage and retrieval system, without prior written permission from Empire Books.

Library of Congress Cataloging-in-Publication Data

ISBN 10: 1-933901-19-5
ISBN 13: 978-1-933901-19-0

Library of Congress Cataloging-in-Publication Data

Magno, Renato, 1962-
  Masterclass Brazilian jiu jitsu : ultimate choking techniques / by Renato Magno. -- 1st ed.
     p. cm.
  Includes index.
  ISBN 1-933901-19-5 (pbk. : alk. paper)
   1. Jiu-jitsu--Brazil. I. Title. II. Title: Brazilian jiu jitsu. III. Title: Jiu jitsu.
  GV1114.S274 2006
  796.815'2--dc22
                                            2006009376

Empire Books
P.O. Box 491788
Los Angeles, CA 90049
(818) 767-7900

First edition
07 06 05 04 03 02 01 00 99 98 97 1 3 5 7 9 10 8 6 4 2
Printed in the United States of America.

Editor: David Tadman
Action Photography: Tom Fitzpatrick
Interior Photography: Jason Alan
Interior & Cover Design: Mario M. Rodriguez, MMR Design Solutions

I dedicate this book to my family with thanks for their support, patience, and love.

ACKNOWLEDGEMENT

Many fine people deserve thanks for helping to put this book together:

To Ricardo Wilker for helping me to illustrate all the techniques.

To Jason Alan, for the numerous hours in front of the camera to capture all the technical details.

To Tom Kellen, editor of the work, for his superb skills.

To Mario Rodriguez for devoting time, passion, and talent in designing the artwork.

And finally, to all those with the courage to take a stand.

ABOUT THE AUTHOR

RENATO MAGNO

Originally from Sao Paulo, Brazil, Renato Magno began his martial arts training in Judo, but Brazilian Jiu Jitsu was what turned his life around. Lucky enough to spend time and train extensively with several members of the Gracie family in Rio de Janeiro, he became an active competitor with an impressive list of accomplishments. In keeping with his reputation of a top Jiu Jitsu man, he displays all the traits of a true martial artist. Out of dedication, he spends long hours on the mat trying to pass on the knowledge of his beloved art to his numerous students at various Machado Jiu Jitsu schools in Southern California.

"No question is too insignificant to ask," says Magno. "If someone wants me to explain a position, it is because they don't understand it. I'm glad to have the knowledge that enables me to help someone. Being an instructor is as much about how you relate as it is about how much you know. You can have the best techniques in the world, but if you don't know how to get your point across, then your knowledge is worthless."

No matter how refined his Jiu Jitsu techniques are, however, Magno recognizes the need for versatility. "No modern martial art is a complete system in itself. It's very important for grapplers to understand the striking aspects of combat," he says. "If you don't know how to defend against strikes, someone is going to hit you and knock you out. But if you know how to defend against them, then you can take a person down and grapple." This realistic approach has caused Renato Magno to be widely regarded as one of the top Brazilian Jiu Jitsu instructors in the world.

TABLE OF CONTENTS

Introduction ix

Types of Chokes 1
Cross Choke 2
Reversed Cross Choke 4
Basic Cross Choke 6
Naked Choke - Method A 8
Naked Choke - Method B 9
Far Arm Choke 10
Single Arm Choke 12

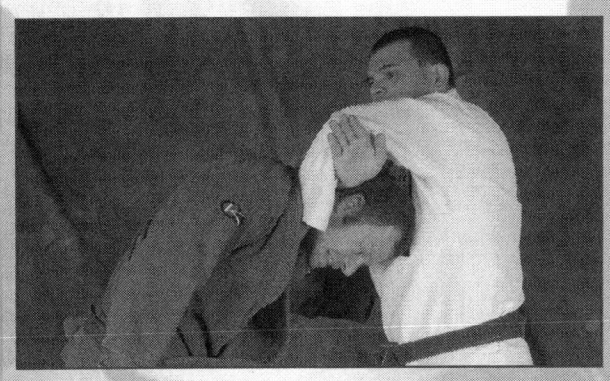

Standing Chokes 14
From the Front 16
From the Back. 38

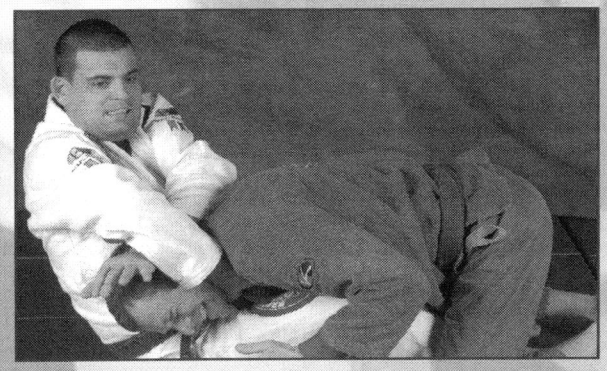

Ground Chokes 48
Seating 50
From the Side 72
From the Guard 122
From the Back 136
From the Mount 158
Facing the Guard 166

Conclusion .176

INTRODUCTION

Choking the opponent is one of the trademarks of Brazilian Jiu Jitsu and it is considered by many as the "most human and merciful" submission technique in the fighting arts. Royce Gracie opened the eyes of millions of martial artists to the effectiveness of the choking techniques when, in 1993, he became the first champion of the UFC event. By simply mounting and controlling his opponents, he was capable of submitting them with a merciful Jiu Jitsu technique, giving them always the opportunity to "tap" publicly as a sign of defeat. His older brother Rickson Gracie traveled to Japan and did the same in Pride FC. The Japanese audience was shocked to see Gracie defeating bigger and stronger opponents by applying a rear naked choke.

The proper training and use of choking techniques requires more attention to detail than many other skills in the art. Using the choking techniques of BJJ will give the practitioner a variety of finishes to any situation he may find himself in, self-defense or sport competition.

The whole idea behind choking your opponent is to cut off his air supply, which basically causes him to tap or pass out—if the opponent is stubborn enough to acknowledge and accept the inevitable. The action of choking can be divided into two different methods:

1) The carotid artery choke, in which pressure is applied to the carotid artery, sealing off the flow of blood and oxygen to the brain. We apply the pressure to the side of the neck, sandwiching the artery between the biceps and the forearm, and occa-

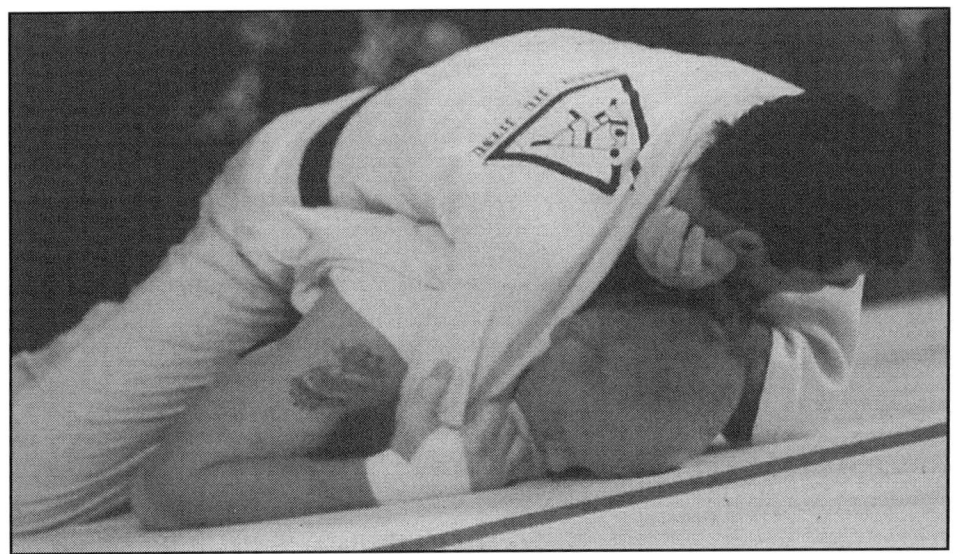

Introduction

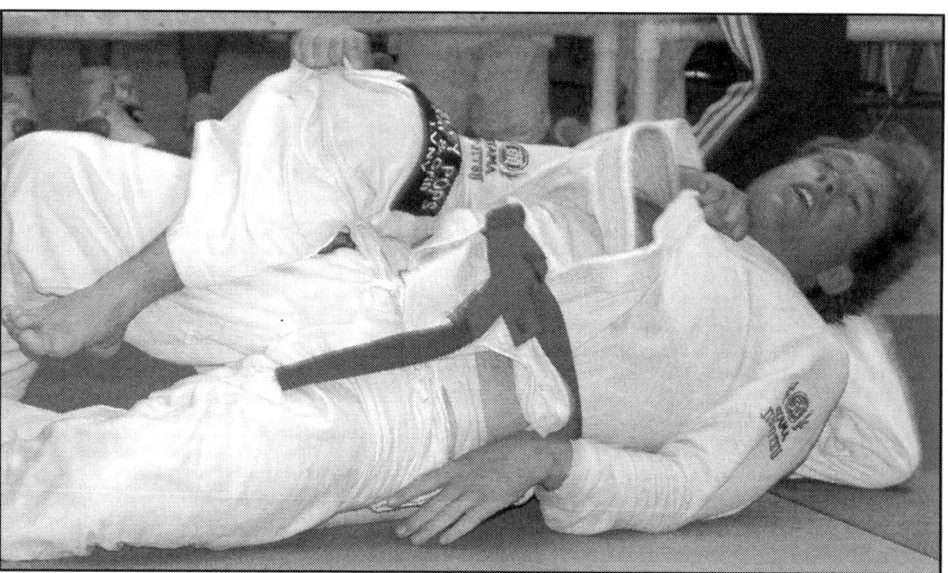

sionally using the opponent's arm to increase the pressure. This causes the opponent to pass out (it takes approximately six to eight seconds to accomplish). Holding the choke much longer—20 second or more—will possibly cause brain damage. Holding the choke longer than this can cause death.

2) The windpipe choke. Here pressure is applied from the front of the neck to the back The pressure applied to the windpipe causes the flow of air to the lungs to be shut off. Too much pressure on the esophagus will cause it to collapse. The obvious end result would be the possibility of the opponent choking to death unless proper medical attention is administered in a short period of time.

There is another method of "choking" the opponent and it is based on the compression of the chest and lungs, preventing him from inhaling. This method is more difficult to apply, although is extensively used in other grappling arts like Judo when one of the fighters has the weight advantage.

From this basic description of how a choke works in combat, we can easily see the options at hand. In a sport competition, the final submission technique is to choke your opponent; from a self-defense point of view, using a choking technique can clam your aggressor down and take the steam out of someone who is uncontrollable without seriously hurting him.

The first method—using the compression of the carotid arteries—is more desirable because it requires the least force, although it demands an exact and proper technique in the delivery of the action. This involves less pain and is safer to apply than those chokes that directly attack the windpipe or trachea.

Chokes can be applied with the arms, but also with the proper use of the legs. The "triangle choke" is a good example of how a skilled BJJ practitioner doesn't need to use his hands to apply pressure on his opponent's neck; he can finish him off with the use of his legs.

Many people mistake the choking techniques with other attacks called "neck cranks." A neck crank is not a choke but a "joint lock" that momentarily reduces the air supply and mainly works because the hyperextension occurred in the neck area.

One important tactical aspects of choking is to use an indirect approach in our method of attack. Don't go "directly" for the choke, since this will be very obvious and your opponent will prevent the attempt. Therefore, set your choke by attacking the arms first. Make your opponent believe that you are "working" for an arm-lock and strategically place your hands in a position that, with very little modification, you will be able to apply a finishing choke. When applying the choke, if you do not choke with as narrow as possible part of the arm, the efficacy of the lock will be impaired. Your strangling arm should be used like a soft rope around your opponent's neck and throat. When you are choking the opponent, unless you are in a position that enables your own body to be adequately managed, you will not only be unable to control your opponent but your bodily strength that passes through your arm to strangle your opponent cannot be properly utilized.

A simple bit of advice for your training: if your training partner gets a clean grip on the technique, don't try to be macho. Simply tap and let him know he accomplished a good technique. The idea of "not-tapping" when

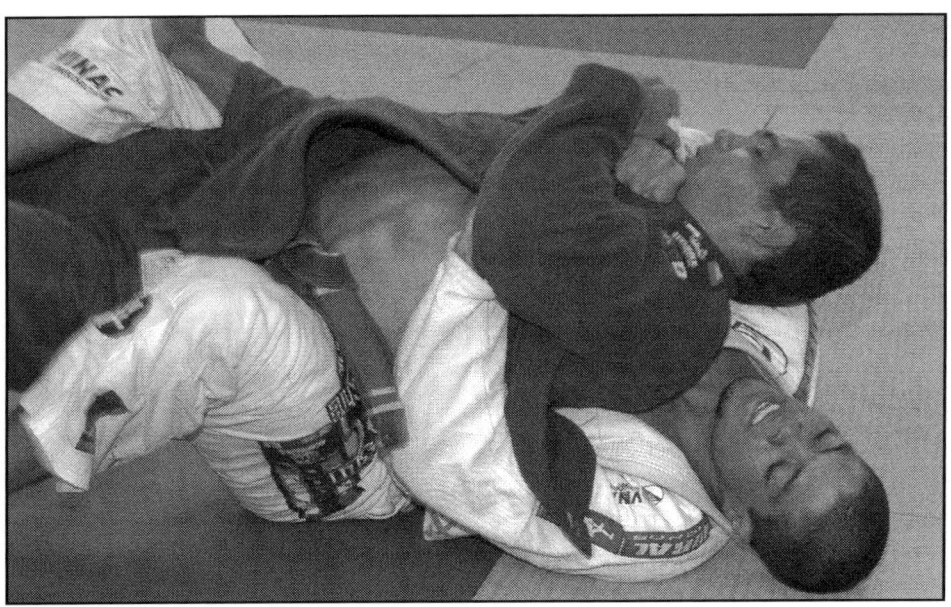

INTRODUCTION

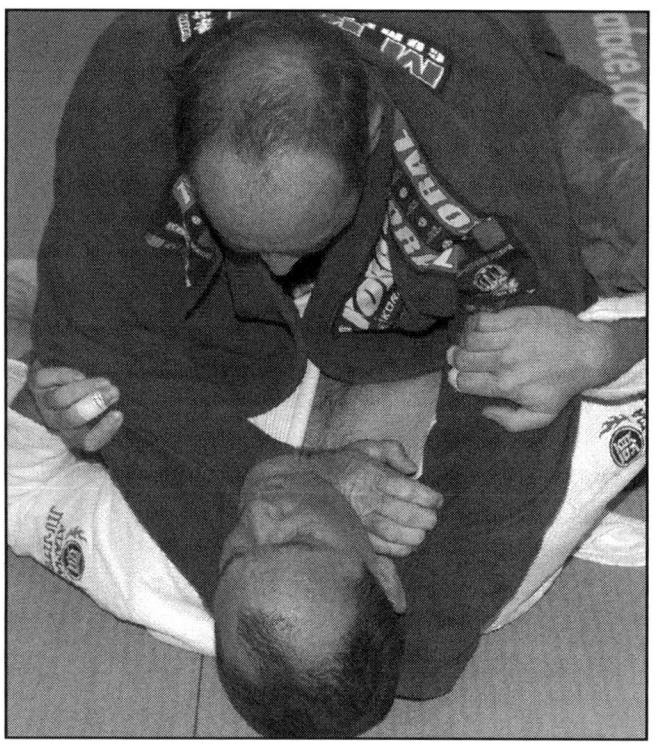

someone gets you in a clean choking technique is simply stupid. Train hard, but train safely...this is the only way to really improve in your Brazilian Jiu Jitsu game.

SAFETY RULES

Release pressure immediately when the opponent submits. Be sensitive enough to feel when the opponent is almost ready to pass out, so you can immediately release the pressure. You should have enough control of the situation that you feel the lack of body resistance to your technique when the opponent is not capable of resisting. As the choke takes effect, the opponent may breathe stertorously, and often his body will jerk convulsively.

Always know when to "give up" and stop fighting against a choke technique being applied to you. Learn to recognize when the opponent has a submission choke on you and there is no chance for you to escape. Tap when you feel there is no escape...but don't wait too long or your opponent will keep the pressure until you lose your consciousness. It is far better that you should let go too soon in the mistaken belief that your opponent has submitted than hold on too long in the mistaken belief that he is still resisting. Many people still think that an honorable way of dealing with a choking technique is to resist it until unconsciousness occurs. Definitely, we don't support this practice.

Train and practice all the choking techniques under the proper supervision of a qualified instructor in Brazilian Jiu Jitsu. Don't "play" by yourself without complete knowledge of how to apply pressure and how to resuscitate your partner in case an accident happens. Choking techniques are potentially fatal and should be treated seriously.

Although many choking techniques can be applied from a standing position, start practicing them on the ground. This will reduce the risk of injuries due to the fact the leverage and body weight during ground practice is more controllable than when practicing from a standing position.

Tips

- Always be in a secure advantageous position where your moves are unrestricted.

- Complete relaxation is the key in all choking techniques. Unless your arms are fully relaxed, they cannot be made to "fit" the shape of your opponent's neck. Excessive tension will cause your opponent pain, though it will place him in no danger of strangulation.

- Have the principles of mechanical leverage in mind so you can use your strength to a maximum.

- Make sure your body has complete freedom of movement so that you are in the best position to apply the technique and to stop any of the opponent's attempts to escape.

- When executing the choke, decide where to apply it and what method of application to use in order to achieve the greatest efficiency and results in the shortest possible time.

- Practice the techniques without resistance from your partner until the reactions become natural and instinctive.

- Train your hand to get an accurate hold the minute you begin the technique. Constantly having to adjust the grip will give the opponent more opportunities to counter the attack.

- The entire body, not only the hands and wrist, should be used in a gentle but firm way to complete the choking technique.

- Use the smaller sides of the wrists when you apply the technique. The wrists should be flexible and used so as to act like a pliable rope around the neck. Don't allow any space between the neck and the arms, hands, and wrists. The opportunity to apply a choke in a real confrontation can be lost in one second.

- The key is constancy of pressure rather than extreme force. Don't rely on excessive force since very little, but properly applied, pressure is all that it takes to compress the artery and render the opponent unconscious.

TYPES OF CHOKES

There are various and complex varieties in the methods used to choke the opponent out, but the ones described in this chapter involve the basic and fundamental principles used in any other variations. Study and master these since they are the foundation of all choking possibilities in the art of Brazilian Jiu Jitsu.

Cross Choke 2
Reverse Crossed Choke 4
Basic Cross Choke 6
Naked Choke - Method A 8
Naked Choke - Method A 9
Far Collar Choke 10
Single Arm Choke 12

TYPES OF CHOKES

CROSS CHOKE

This is the simplest and most basic choke to learn, but the most important of all since will teach you the basic principles that you'll end up using in the other variables.

The ease of application and the relatively short time to accomplish its effect makes this choke a valuable one not only for a beginner student but also for the advanced practitioner. There are three variations of this choke depending on the position of the hands, but all of them follow the same principles of application.

In the practical application of this choke, both lapels of the opponent are gripped from the front. The wrists cross over in front of the neck, and pressure is applied to both sides of the neck, specifically to the carotid and to the jugular vein.

Description: With the right hand, grasp the right side of the opponent's collar (fingers inside the jacket, thumb out), with the small finger against the opponent's jugular vein. With the left hand, grasp the left side of the opponent's collar (fingers in, thumb out), with the small finger against the opponent's carotid artery. Apply pressure consistently.

TIPS

Grasp the collar with both hands so that the four fingers on the inside are placed against the jugular vein and the carotid artery.

When tightening up for the choke, imagine that your small fingers are to touch one another. If the opponent rolls to the side, roll over with him and scissor his body with your legs to maintain control of him.

Add the body weight to reinforce the strength of the arms and hands in choking.

Practice with much repetition, grasping the collar quickly.

A

B

C

D

TYPE OF CHOKES

TYPES OF CHOKES

REVERSE CROSSED CHOKE

A

B

In the application of this choke, both lapels of the opponent are gripped from the front as in the previous technique. The wrists cross over in front of the neck, and pressure is applied to both sides of the neck, to the jugular vein and carotid artery.

Description: With the right hand, grasp the right side of the opponent's collar (fingers inside the jacket, thumb out), with the small finger against the opponent's jugular vein. The left hand, either circles over the top of the opponent's head from left to right in a half-circle, or directly moves in front of the opponent's face to grasp his right side of the collar (thumb in, fingers out). The small finger of the left hand is placed against the opponent's carotid artery. Then pull and twist the left hand to the left. The outside small part of the right wrist and forearm is placed against opponent's throat (larynx). Both hands are pulled, then squeezed or wrenched tightly, at the neck.

TIPS

Clamp opponent's body tightly with your legs and feet to control his movements.

Practice with many repetitions, grasping the collar quickly and efficiently with both hands.

The right hand should firmly grasp the opponent's right collar.

For further pointers, refer to those under "cross choke."

C

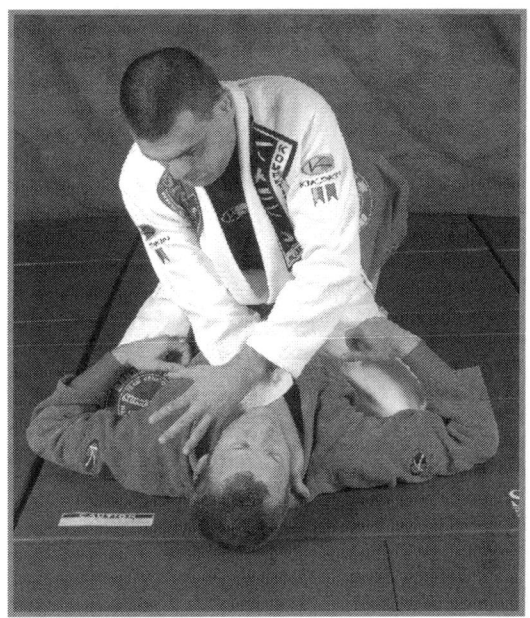
D

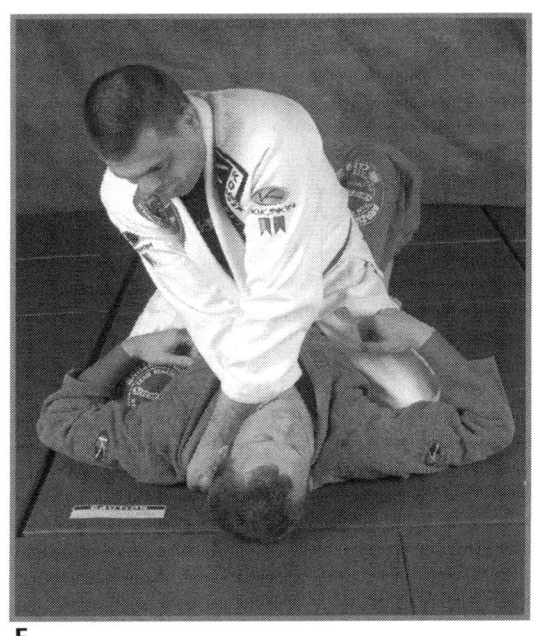
E

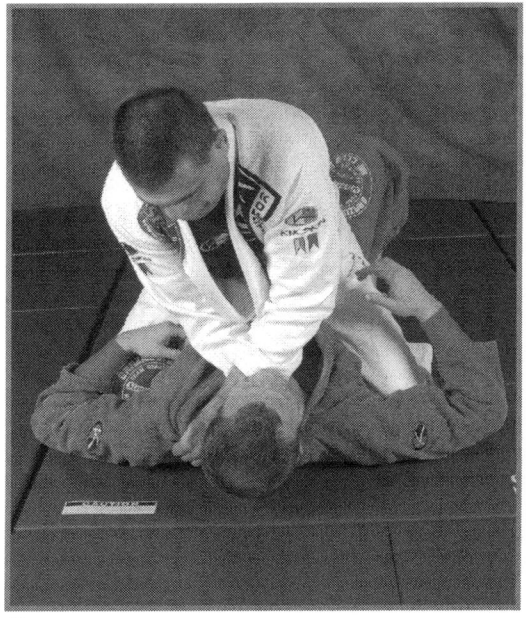
F

TYPE OF CHOKES

TYPES OF CHOKES

BASIC CROSS CHOKE

A

The methods of application in this technique are identical to the two previous techniques, except that the hand grip is directly reversed from that of the latter choke.

Description: Both hands grasp opponent's collar with the thumb in and the fingers out. The left wrist crosses over the right wrist. The lateral sides of both wrists are placed against the opponent's jugular vein and carotid artery.

TIPS

The second hand used in the technique may also grasp the opponent's shoulder to apply the choking technique.
Refer to pointers under Cross Choke and Reverse Cross Choke

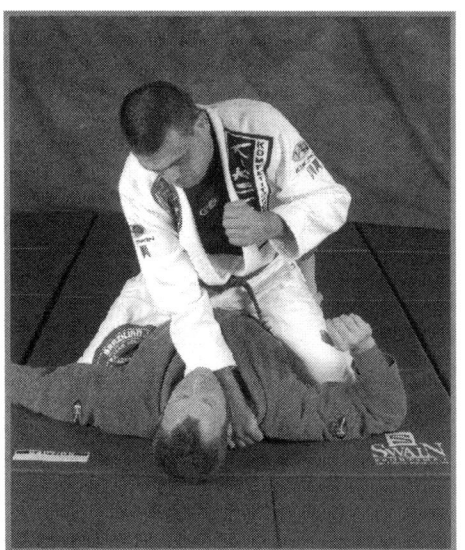
B

C

D

E

TYPE OF CHOKES

TYPES OF CHOKES

NAKED CHOKE - METHOD A

This choking technique is applied without the use of the gi and it has two important variables. The first method applies pressure on the opponent's carotid artery and jugular vein.

Description: Your left arm goes over the opponent's left shoulder and the medial side of your forearm is placed against the opponent's side of the neck. Your arm should snugly circle the opponent's neck, with the tip of the elbow pointing down directly under the opponent's chin. The right arm goes behind the back of the opponent's head, and the palm of this hand is placed on his head. Close and pull the left hand and arm, and push with the right hand. Use the chest expanding to increase pressure.

A

> **TIPS**
>
> This method of applying the choke requires a little more time than previous techniques.
> However, once it is applied, it is more effective than other methods would be.

B

C

NAKED CHOKE - METHOD B

The lateral part of the wrist is applied directly to the neck without the use of the gi. This technique is applied from the front of the neck by putting pressure on the windpipe with the medial part of the wrist and choking. Once the choke takes effect, there is a certain amount of danger to the larynx.

Description: The left arm reaches over the opponent's left shoulder and the medial part of the lower forearm is placed against the opponent's throat. The palm of the hand is down, and the hand is placed as far as the opponent's right shoulder. The right hand, palm up, is placed over the opponent's shoulder and under the left hand, where the two hands are clasped together. The left shoulder is placed in the back of the opponent's head for added pressure and support. Your left cheek should be placed against the right side of the opponent's face.

A

TIPS

Pressure is applied against the opponent's windpipe directly from the front.
Attacker securely tightens the hand grip by placing his right shoulder against the back of the opponent's head.
Very little time is required for the applications of this technique due to the simplicity of its maneuver.

B

C

TYPE OF CHOKES

Types of Chokes

FAR COLLAR CHOKE

This choke is known to be one of the most effective of the choking techniques in the arsenal of Brazilian Jiu Jitsu. Its high efficiency makes this technique very popular during training and in competition. There are many opportunities to use this technique and it is a perfect base from which to go into other techniques. It is applied from behind the opponent's back. The pressure is applied on three areas simultaneously: the jugular vein, the carotid artery, and the windpipe. This technique can be developed to such a high level of efficiency that once the attacker moves behind the opponent, there is very little chance of the latter escaping.

Description: The left hand grasp the opponent's right collar deeply (thumb in, fingers out) and the medial part of the lower forearm and wrist are wrapped around the opponent's jugular vein and the front of his neck. The right hand goes under the opponent's right armpit and slips under your own left wrist to grasp the left side of the collar (thumb in, fingers out). The left hand is pulled to the left rear, and the right hand is pulled down and to the right. Both hands squeeze tightly, and the choke is applied.

> **TIPS**
> The right hand should grasp the opponent's collar deeply. The forearm and the jacket act as a noose around the opponent's neck.
> If time permits, and in order to grasp the opponent's left collar deeply, use the left hand to pull down on the front of that collar, then grasp high and deeply on it with the right hand.

A

B

C

D

TYPES OF CHOKES

SINGLE ARM CHOKE

This technique has features similar to those of the previous one. This choking action is frequently used as a continuation of the Far Collar Choke. Although this technique is not in frequent use, if one can learn to use it properly, it can be very helpful in many situations. The choke is applied from behind the opponent and only one of the collars is grasped, with one of the arms being contained overhead. The pressure is applied to the jugular vein, the carotid artery and the windpipe simultaneously.

Description: The left hand grasps the opponent's right collar deeply (thumb in, fingers out) and the medial part of the lower forearm and wrist are wrapped around opponent's jugular vein and the front of his neck. The right hand goes under the opponent's right armpit and lifts the opponent's right arm directly overhead. Then apply control by reaching way over to the left, overlapping the left wrist with the right wrist, and place the palm of the right hand against the back of the opponent's neck.

TIPS

The opponent's left hand and arm must be lifted high and to the left for the arm to be controlled.

The left hand, which goes against the back of the opponent's head, may, at times, be pushed underneath the right wrist instead of on the top of it.

If opportunity permits, to ensure a deep grasp with the right hand, you may first use your left hand to grip the opponent's left lapel from under the left armpit, and then take a deep hold on his left collar.

A

B

C

D

STANDING CHOKES

From the Front 16
From the Back 38

Standing Chokes

FROM THE FRONT

1. Renato reaches the opponent's left side of the collar and pulls to open space.

2. Then, he brings his left hand inside the collar (palm up), making sure he reaches all the way in.

TECHNIQUE 1

3. Now he brings his right hand (palm up) and passes it under the left hand. Renato reaches the inside of the right side of the opponent's collar.

4. When he has secured a tight grip with both hands, he pulls the opponent into his chest and applies a front choke.

Standing Chokes

FROM THE FRONT

1. With his left hand, Renato reaches the opponent's left side of the collar and pulls to open space. Then, he brings his left hand inside the collar (palm up), making sure he reaches all the way in.

2. Now, he puts his right hand over his left hand with the palm down...

Technique 2

3. ...And grabs the opponent's right side of the collar.

4. Then, he brings both of his elbows down close to the body and chokes his opponent.

STANDING CHOKES

FROM THE FRONT

1. With his left hand, Renato reaches the opponent's left side of the collar and pulls to open space. Then, he brings his left hand inside the collar (palm up), making sure he reaches all the way in...

2. ...and pulls hard to bring the opponent's head down with the help of his right hand.

TECHNIQUE 3

3. Now, he passes his right hand behind the opponent's neck...

4. ...and, pulling with his left hand, applies a finishing choke.

STANDING CHOKES

STANDING CHOKES

FROM THE FRONT

1. With his left hand, Renato reaches the opponent's left side of the collar and pulls to open space. Then, he brings his left hand inside the collar (palm up), making sure he reaches all the way in...

2. ...and brings his right hand to the left side of the opponent's neck. With his palm down, he inserts his thumb inside the collar.

TECHNIQUE 4

3. Then, he moves his hand in a circle to the left, passing his right elbow over the opponent's head...

4. ...and closes the grip to apply a frontal choke.

STANDING CHOKES

FROM THE FRONT

1. Renato faces his opponent and grabs the collar of the gi with both hands.

2. Then, he leans forward and brings the opponent's left side of the collar close to the left so he can grab it with his left hand.

TECHNIQUE 5

3. By pulling up, Renato applies a finishing choke to his opponent.

STANDING CHOKES

FROM THE FRONT

1. The opponent grabs Renato's left lapel.

2. Renato brings his left arm around the opponent's right arm...

3. ...and grabs the opponent's left side of the collar with his left hand.

TECHNIQUE 6

4. With his right hand, Renato grabs the opponent's right shoulder and applies a front choke.

STANDING CHOKES

FROM THE FRONT

1. The opponent grabs Renato's left lapel.

2. Description of the move Description of the moveDescription of the moveDescription of the moveDescription of the move

3. ...brings his left arm around the opponent's right arm.

4. Then, he grabs the opponent's left side of the collar with his left hand.

TECHNIQUE 7

5. Now, Renato grabs the opponent's left side of the collar with his right hand (palm down).

6. He brings his right elbow up and passes the arm around the neck...

7. ...to apply a frontal choke.

STANDING CHOKES

STANDING CHOKES

FROM THE FRONT

1. Renato reaches with his left the opponent left side of the collar and pulls to open space. Then, he brings his left hand inside the collar (palm-up), making sure he reaches all the way in…

2. …and pulls hard to bring the opponent's head down with the help of his right hand.

Technique 8

3. With his opponent leaning forward, Renato passes his right hand in front of the opponent's left arm...

4. ...and applies a front choke by putting his right arm between the opponent's neck and left arm.

STANDING CHOKES

FROM THE FRONT

1. Renato Magno faces his opponent.

2. Renato brings his left arm around the left side of the opponent's neck and...

TECHNIQUE 9

3. ...wraps it around the neck...

4. until he can reach and grab his own right hand. Then, he pulls up and applies a finishing frontal choke.

STANDING CHOKES

FROM THE FRONT

1. Renato, with his right hand, grabs his opponent's left side of the collar.

2. By pulling with his right hand, Renato opens space to bring his left hand inside the collar with the palm facing up.

3. Then, he passes his right hand (with the palm facing up) under his left and reaches the other side of the collar.

TECHNIQUE 10

4. Now, Renato gets closer to the opponent's body…

5. …and puts his legs around the waist, simultaneously dropping his body onto the ground, falling with the opponent inside the guard.

6. Renato pulls hard with both hands and apply a frontal choke.

STANDING CHOKES

FROM THE FRONT

1. Renato grabs his opponent's collar with both hands.

2. Suddenly, he jumps and closes his guard, maintaining his opponent close to him.

3. Now, Renato pulls the left side of the collar with his right hand and inserts his left hand all the way in, with the palm facing up.

TECHNIQUE 11

4. Once the grip with the left hand is secured, Renato passes his right hand under the left and …

5. …secures a tight grip…

6. to apply a finishing choke from the closed guard position.

Standing Chokes

FROM THE BACK

1. Renato approaches his opponent from behind.

2. He brings his left arm around the opponent's neck...

3. ...and closes the action, making sure the arm is tight with the opponent's neck.

TECHNIQUE 1

4. Now that the left arm is tight around the opponent's neck, Renato brings his right arm and places his right hand behind the opponent's head...

5. ...to apply a finishing rear choke.

Standing Chokes

FROM THE BACK

1. Renato approaches his opponent from behind.

2. Now, he brings his right arm under the opponent's right armpit and grabs the right side of the collar.

3. With his right hand, Renato brings the opponent's right side of the collar closer so he can grab it with his left hand that has passed in front of the opponent's neck.

TECHNIQUE 2

4. Then, he secures the grip with his left hand…

5. …and, with the right hand, pulls hard on the left part of the opponent's gi to apply the final choke.

Standing Chokes

FROM THE BACK

1. Renato approaches his opponent from behind.

2. He brings his left arm around the opponent's neck...

3. ...and grabs the right side of the opponent's collar, grabbing the top part of the right shoulder.

Technique 3

4. Then, he brings his right arm behind the opponent's neck...

5. ...and, pulling back, applies a rear choke.

STANDING CHOKES

FROM THE BACK

1. Renato approaches his opponent from behind.

2. He brings both arms under the opponent's arms...

3. ...and pulls them up.

Technique 4

4. Then, he closes the grip behind the opponent's neck...

5. ...and by pulling forward, applies a rear choke.

STANDING CHOKES

FROM THE BACK

1. Renato approaches his opponent from behind.

2. He passes his left hand in front the opponent's face...

3. ...to reach the left side of the neck in a wrapping motion.

TECHNIQUE 5

4. Once the arm has passed and wrapped the opponent's neck, Renato grabs his left wrist with his right hand…

5. …and pulls back hard to apply a final rear choke.

GROUND CHOKES

Seating 50

From the Side 72

From the Guard 122

From the Back 136

From the Mount 158

Facing the Guard 166

GROUND CHOKES

SEATING

1. Renato, seated, is facing his opponent.

2. Renato grabs the opponent's right sleeve with his right hand.

3. Then, he pulls back while simultaneously inserting his left hand under the opponent's arm...

4. ...to grab the left collar.

TECHNIQUE 1

5. Then, he brings his right hand and grabs the collar with the thumb in and the palm down.

6. Now, Renato lifts his elbow, circles it around the opponent's head...

7. ...and brings it to the front...

8. from where he applies a final choke.

GROUND CHOKES
SEATING

1. Renato faces his opponent from a seated position.

2. Using his right hand, Renato open space to put his left hand inside the opponent's collar.

3. Then, he brings his right hand under his left arm and reaches for the other side of the opponent's collar.

TECHNIQUE 2

4. Once both grips are deep and secure…

5. …Renato pulls with both arms and simultaneously pushes away with his feet to create extra pressure on the neck while he applies a finishing choke.

GROUND CHOKES

SEATING

1. Renato faces his opponent from a seated position and grabs the opponent's right sleeve with his right hand.

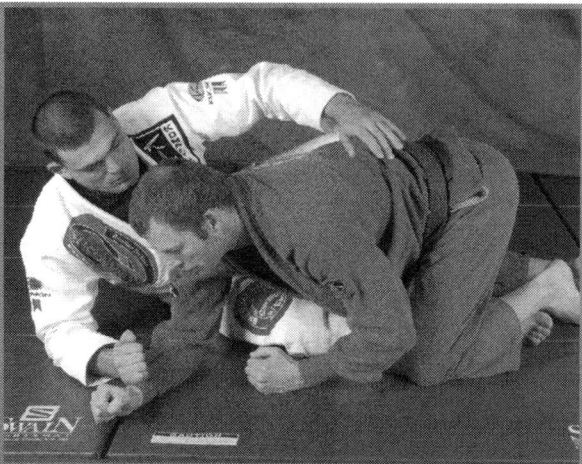

2. He pulls hard and brings the opponent off balance.

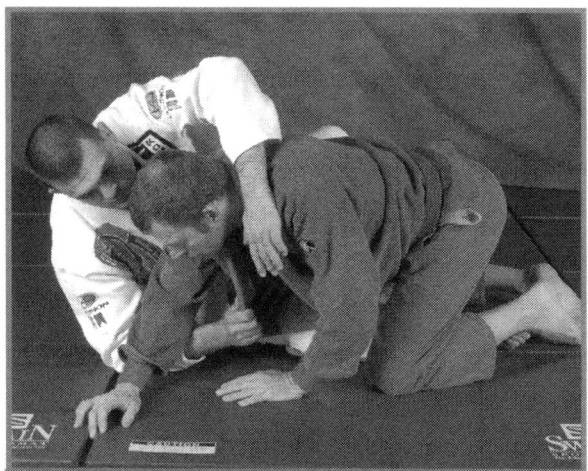

3. Then, he grabs the opponent's collar with his right hand as he simultaneously reaches from behind the neck with his left hand.

4. Now, he uses the left hand to grab the opponent's right side of the collar as he releases the grip with his right hand.

TECHNIQUE 3

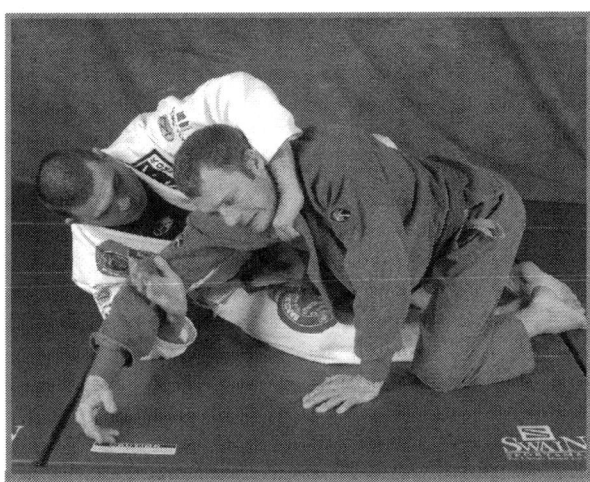

5. Renato, with his right hand, pulls the opponent's right arm away from the body...

6. ...and secures his grip and position on the ground.

7. Then, he applies a final choke by pulling hard with his left and pushing with his right foot on the opponent's left leg.

GROUND CHOKES
SEATING

1. Renato, seated, reaches for the opponent's left side of the collar.

2. Then, he grabs the inside of the collar with his right hand…

3. …and brings the opponent's head down with his left hand…

Technique 4

4. ...to secure the grip...

5. ...as he simultaneously passes his left arm behind the opponent's neck...

6. ...to apply a painful finishing choke.

GROUND CHOKES
SEATING

1. The opponent tries to grab Renato's gi but, with both hands, Renato blocks the grabbing attempt.

2. Then, he takes advantage and secures a grip with his right hand on the left side of the opponent's collar.

3. Once he has created space with his right hand, Renato brings his left hand all the way inside the opponent's collar.

TECHNIQUE 5

4. He passes his right hand under the left arm…

5. …and pulls hard toward himself to apply a frontal choke.

GROUND CHOKES
SEATING

1. Renato, seated, faces his opponent.

2. Using his left hand, Renato brings the opponent's right sleeve closer to him...

3. ...so he can grab it with his right hand...

4. ...to create space, and insert his left hand under the opponent's right armpit to grab the left side of the collar.

TECHNIQUE 6

5. Once the grip with the left hand is secured and tight,

6. Renato brings his right hand over the opponent's right shoulder,

7. grabs the gi and applies a finishing frontal choke.

GROUND CHOKES
SEATING

1. Renato, seated, has the opponent inside his open guard.

2. He brings his left arm to the left side of the opponent's neck...

3. ...and around the back...

4. ...as he simultaneously passes his right arm under the opponent's left armpit.

TECHNIQUE 7

5. Now, he grabs his left wrist with the right hand...

6. ...secures the grip properly...

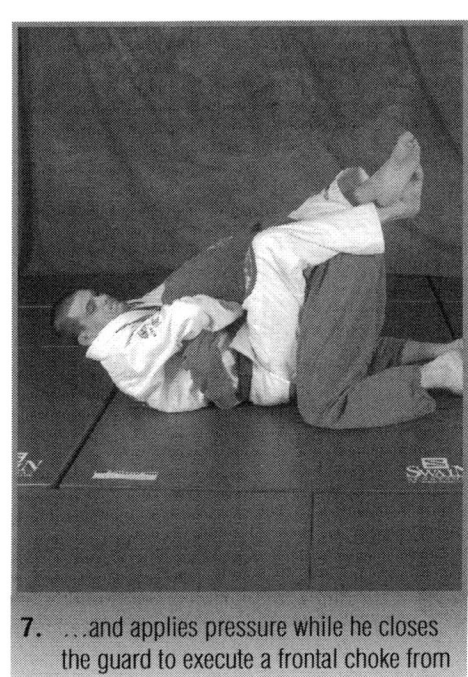

7. ...and applies pressure while he closes the guard to execute a frontal choke from the closed guard.

GROUND CHOKES
SEATING

1. Renato reaches with his left hand for the opponent's left side of the collar.

2. Then, he secures the grip on the opponent's left knee...

3. ...and brings his right leg to the outside to create balance as he simultaneously wraps his left arm around the opponent's neck.

TECHNIQUE 8

4. Now, Renato pulls the opponent's left arm close to his body...

5. ...brings his right knee to the ground...

(CONTINUED ON NEXT PAGE)

GROUND CHOKES

SEATING

(CONTINUED FROM PREVIOUS PAGE)

6. ...and begins to roll over his right shoulder...

7. ...to turn his opponent around and on his back...

8. ...without releasing any of the grips.

TECHNIQUE 8

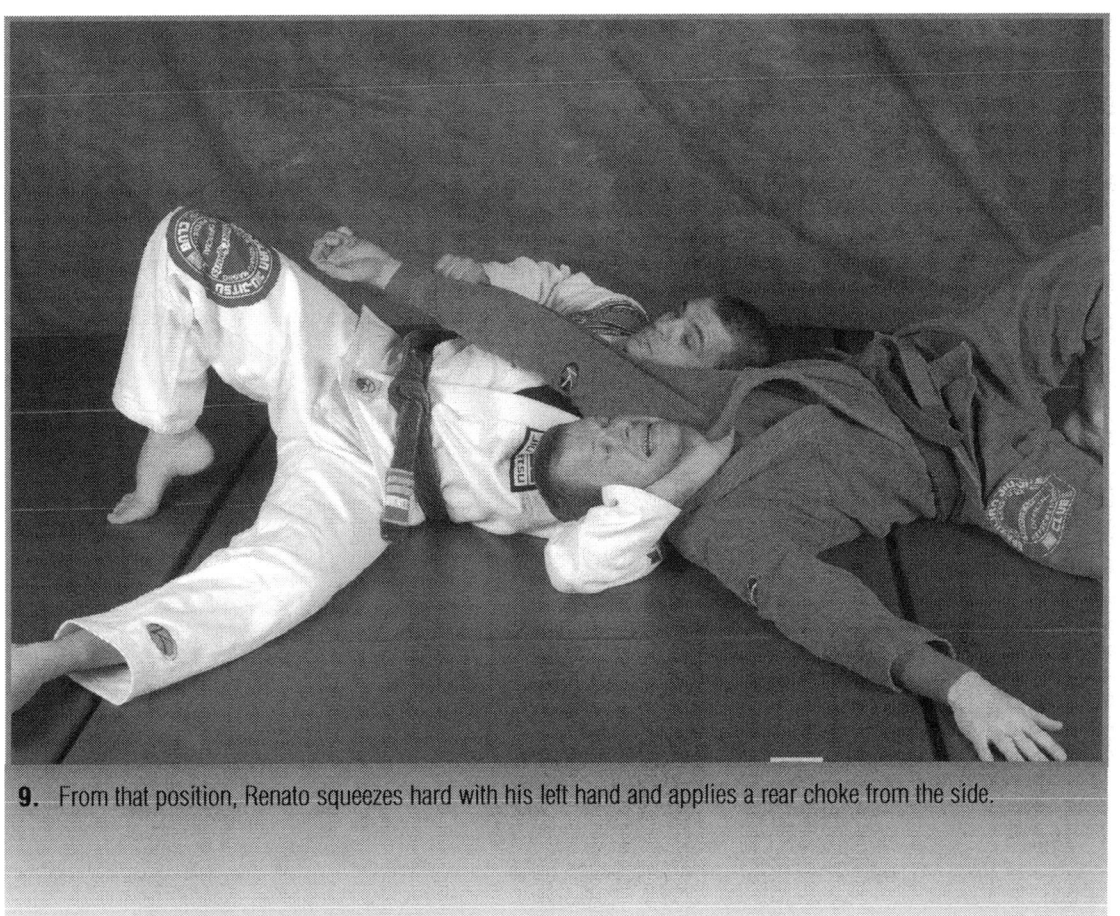

9. From that position, Renato squeezes hard with his left hand and applies a rear choke from the side.

GROUND CHOKES
SEATING

1. Renato faces his opponent...

2. ...who is grabbing Renato's pants at the knee level.

3. Renato reacts by pulling both of the opponent's sleeves hard to break his balance.

TECHNIQUE 9

4. Then, he switches his left grip to the opponent's left side of the collar...

5. ...and his right hand grabs the opponent's pant at the level of the left knee.

(CONTINUED ON NEXT PAGE)

Ground Chokes
SEATING
(continued from previous page)

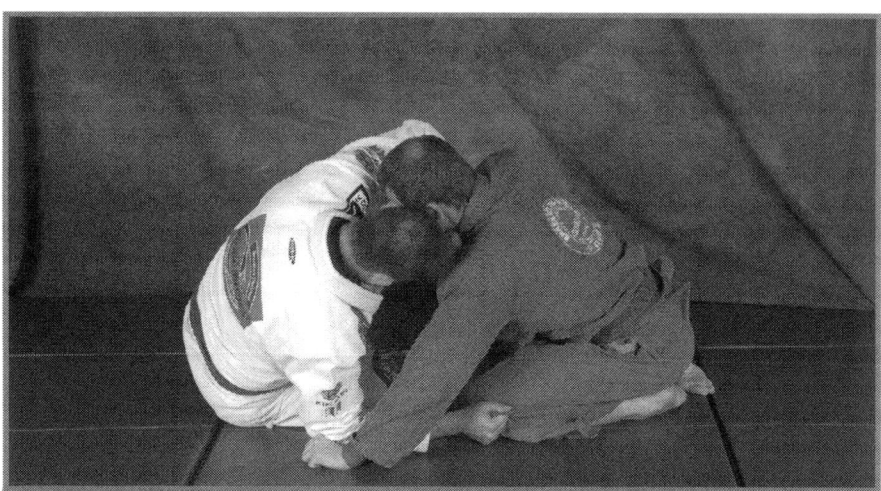

6. Then, he starts turning his body to the right and supports his body on the ground with his right elbow.

7. The left arm begins an upward motion to completely wrap...

TECHNIQUE 9

8. ...the opponent's neck as Renato turns his body on the ground.

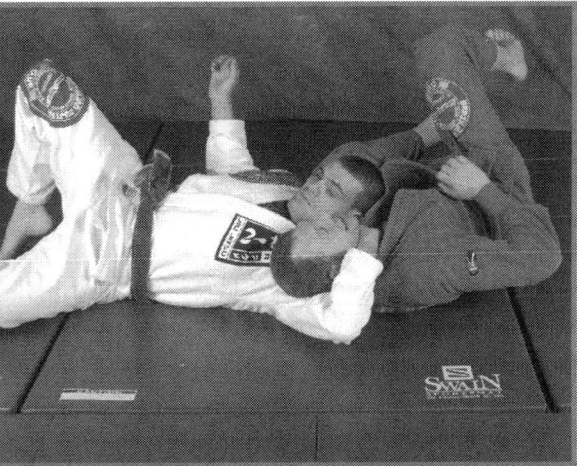

9. With the opponent on his back, and while holding a tight grip with his left hand on the opponent's collar...

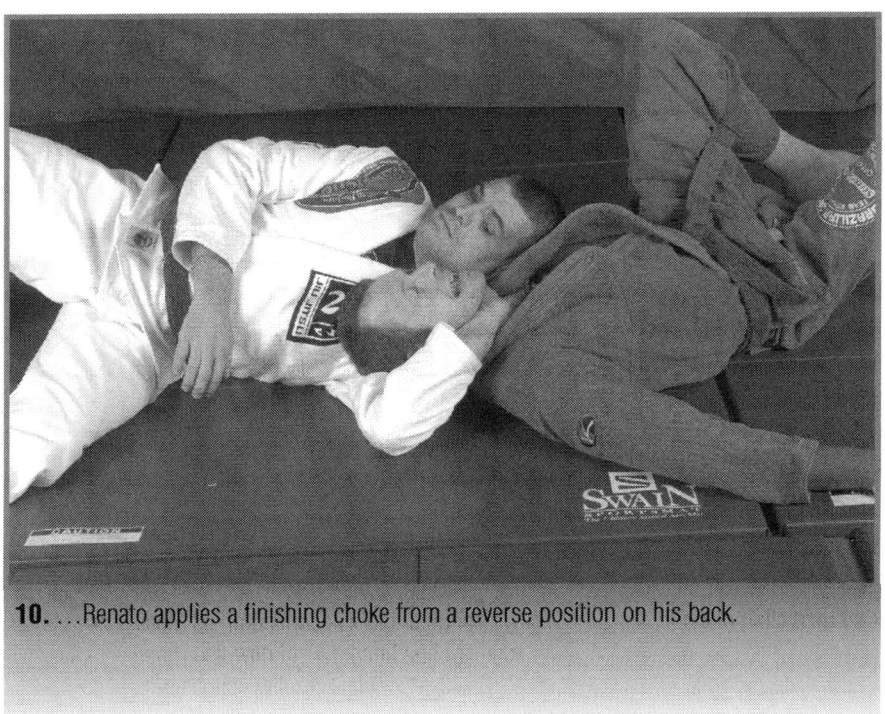

10. ...Renato applies a finishing choke from a reverse position on his back.

GROUND CHOKES

GROUND CHOKES

FROM THE SIDE

1. Renato, on his knees, controls the opponent from the side.

2. With his left hand, Renato pulls hard from the opponent's right side of the collar...

3. ...to create space to insert his right hand (palm up) all the way inside the collar.

TECHNIQUE 1

4. Then, he brings his left hand across the front of the opponent's neck…

5. …to grab the other side of the collar.

6. Once he gets a secure grip with his left hand, he leans forward, closes the left elbow by bringing it down to the ground, and applies a final choke from the side.

GROUND CHOKES
FROM THE SIDE

1. Renato controls the opponent from the side, holding the right side of the collar with his left hand.

2. Now, without releasing the grip, Renato passes his hand behind the opponent's neck to the front in a clockwise motion. This action tightens the collar of the gi around the neck of the opponent.

TECHNIQUE 2

3. Then, he brings his body to the front, moves his left leg backwards, applies pressure with his chest onto the opponent's body, and locks the left elbow to execute a final choke from the side.

GROUND CHOKES

GROUND CHOKES

FROM THE SIDE

1. Renato controls his opponent from the side.

2. Using his left hand, Renato pulls the right side of the opponent's collar to open space.

3. Then, he brings his right hand under the opponent's right arm...

TECHNIQUE 3

4. ...and reaches to grab the collar from under the arm.

5. Once he secures the grip of the collar with the right hand, he passes his left hand in front of the opponent's neck to grab the other side of the collar.

6. Then, he leans forward and, applying pressure, executes a side choke to his opponent.

GROUND CHOKES

FROM THE SIDE

1. Renato is positioned on the right side of his opponent.

2. He leans forward and adopts the side control.

3. Then, he brings his left arm around the opponent's neck in a counterclockwise motion...

TECHNIQUE 4

4. ...until he reaches the front of his left thigh.

5. Now, Renato brings his right hand into action and grabs his left wrist, securing a tight grip.

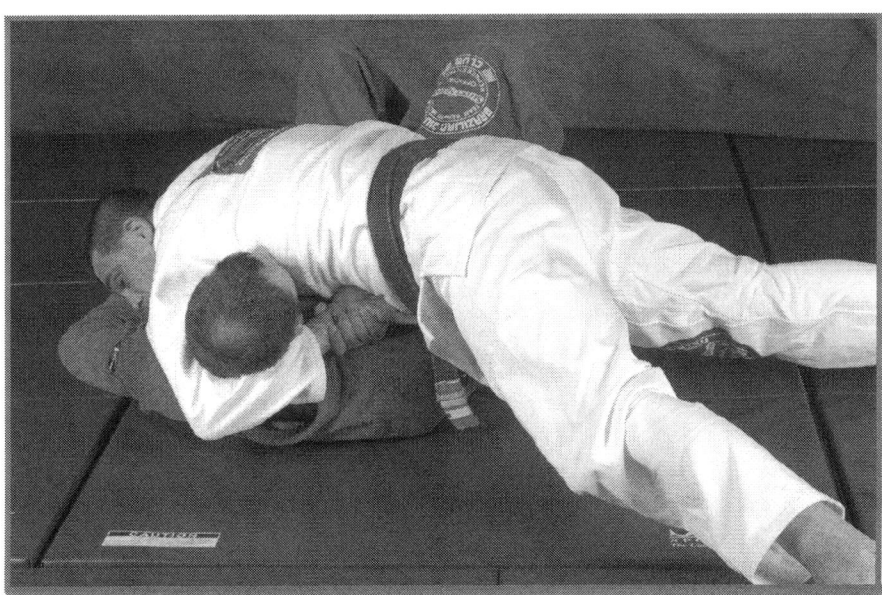

6. To apply the final choke, he leans forward and brings his knees up to put all pressure on the opponent's body as he simultaneously executes the finishing move.

GROUND CHOKES

GROUND CHOKES

FROM THE SIDE

1. Renato controls his opponent with a side knee-on-stomach position.

2. By using his left hand, Renato pulls the left side of the opponent's collar...

3. ...and immediately puts his right hand inside the collar (palm up).

TECHNIQUE 5

4. Then, he begins to move his left hand...

5. ...to grab the opponent's left side of the collar (palm down)...

6. ...and apply a front choke from that position.

GROUND CHOKES

GROUND CHOKES

FROM THE SIDE

1. Renato controls his opponent with a side knee-on-stomach position as he simultaneously uses his right hand to pull the opponent's right sleeve for better control.

2. Now, he passes his left hand under the opponent's right armpit...

3. ...and reaches for the left side of the opponent's collar, inserting his hand all the way in with the palm up.

TECHNIQUE 6

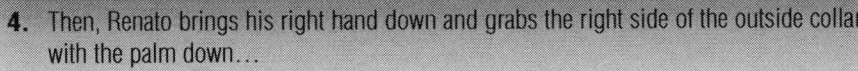

4. Then, Renato brings his right hand down and grabs the right side of the outside collar with the palm down...

5. ...to apply a final frontal choke from the knee-on-stomach position.

GROUND CHOKES

FROM THE SIDE

1. Renato adopts the side control position.

2. The opponent begins to roll to the right side moving away from Renato.

3. Renato keeps the distance close and passes his left arm under the opponent's left armpit...

TECHNIQUE 7

4. ...as he simultaneously reaches for the left side of the opponent's collar with his right hand.

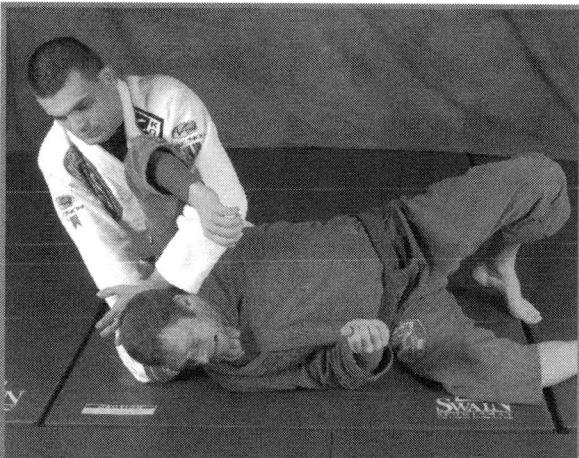

5. Then, he brings his left arm and places it behind the opponent's neck.

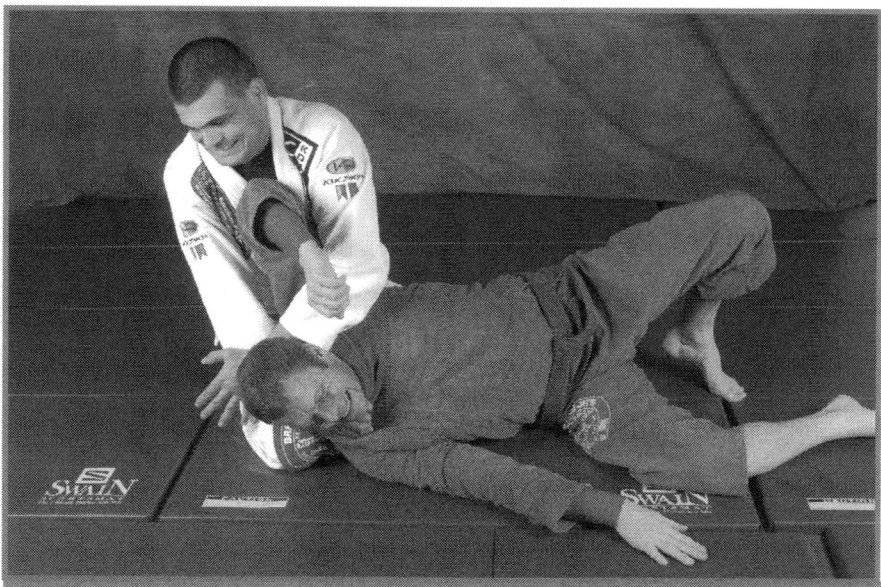

6. By pulling hard with his right hand and applying pressure with his left hand, Renato executes a final choke from the side.

GROUND CHOKES

FROM THE SIDE

1. Renato controls the opponent from the side.

2. The opponent begins to roll to the right side, moving away from Renato.

3. Renato keeps the distance close and passes his left arm under the opponent's left armpit...

TECHNIQUE 8

4. ...as he simultaneously reaches for the left side of the opponent's collar with his right hand.

5. With his left hand, Renato controls the opponent's left hand to prevent him from rolling father away, as he simultaneously brings his right knee and places it behind the opponent's neck.

6. Then, he pushes away with his right knee and pulls back from the collar to choke his opponent out.

GROUND CHOKES

FROM THE SIDE

1. Renato is ready to control the opponent from the side.

2. He leans forward and grabs the opponent's left leg with his left hand as he simultaneously brings his right hand behind the opponent's neck.

TECHNIQUE 9

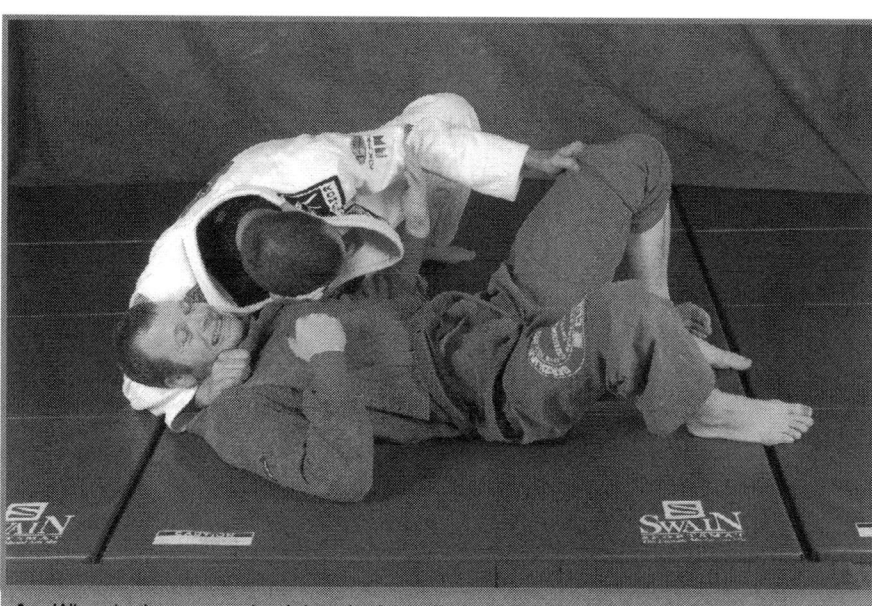

3. Then, he reaches with his right hand all the way around the opponent's neck to grab the left side of the opponent's collar.

4. When he has secured a tight grip, he pulls back hard with his right hand and applies a choke from the side.

GROUND CHOKES

GROUND CHOKES

FROM THE SIDE

1. Renato has the opponent under control from the side. He grabs the tip of the jacket of his gi…

2. …and leans forward to support himself with the left hand on the other side of the opponent's body.

Technique 10

3. Then, he wraps the tip of the jacket around the opponent's neck...

4. ...and brings back the elbow close to the ground to apply a choke with the tip of the gi.

GROUND CHOKES
FROM THE SIDE

1. Renato is on the left side of the opponent.

2. He brings his right hand down and places it inside the opponent's left side of the collar, but uses a reverse grip (palm up facing him).

Technique 11

3. Then, he brings his elbow down to the other side of the opponent's neck and leans forward to apply pressure...

4. ...and finishes his opponent with a one-hand choke.

GROUND CHOKES
FROM THE SIDE

1. Renato is ready to attack his opponent from the side position.

2. He grabs the tip of the opponent's jacket with his left hand...

TECHNIQUE 12

3. ...and passes it to the right hand. Once in the right hand, he wraps it around the right side of the opponent's neck...

4. ...to apply a gi-choke with only one hand.

GROUND CHOKES

FROM THE SIDE

1. Renato is controlling his opponent from the side position.

2. He brings his left hand to the left side of the opponent's collar to open space...

3. ...to insert his right hand inside the collar.

TECHNIQUE 13

4. Renato now brings his right hand around the outside of the opponent's head in a circular motion, without releasing the grip, and ends up with his forearm on the front of the opponent's neck.

5. From this position, Renato leans forward to apply pressure with his body and brings his right elbow to the ground, which creates a front choke to finish his opponent.

GROUND CHOKES

FROM THE SIDE

1. Renato, on the side, is ready to attack the opponent.

2. Renato grabs the tip of his jacket with his right hand...

3. ...and passes it around the right side of the opponent's neck.

TECHNIQUE 14

4. Now, he grabs it with his left hand from the other side…

5. …and begins to lean sideways with his body to apply pressure on the opponent's position.

6. Then, he pulls hard on the gi with his left hand and applies a side choke with the gi.

GROUND CHOKES

FROM THE SIDE

1. Renato is controlling his opponent from the side position.

2. He brings his left leg up and puts his left foot inside the opponent's left leg.

3. Then, Renato begins to apply pressure with his body by slightly leaning forward with his hips.

4. Now, he brings his right leg over the opponent's back and hooks his right foot inside the opponent's right thigh.

Technique 15

5. Renato now push forward with the hips, which makes the opponent's position collapse.

6. He brings his left arm around the opponent's neck...

7. ...places the right arm placed behind the opponent's head...

8. ...and applies a rear choke to finish off his opponent.

GROUND CHOKES
FROM THE SIDE

1. Renato is ready to attack his opponent from the side.

2. Then, Renato puts his left leg inside the opponent's left arm...

3. Then, Renato puts his left leg inside the opponent's left arm...

4. ...as he begins to apply pressure, and grabs the right side of the collar with his left hand from the front of the neck...

Technique 16

5. ...before initiating the rolling action over the opponent's back.

6. Once Renato has landed on the other side of the opponent's body, and without releasing the grips...

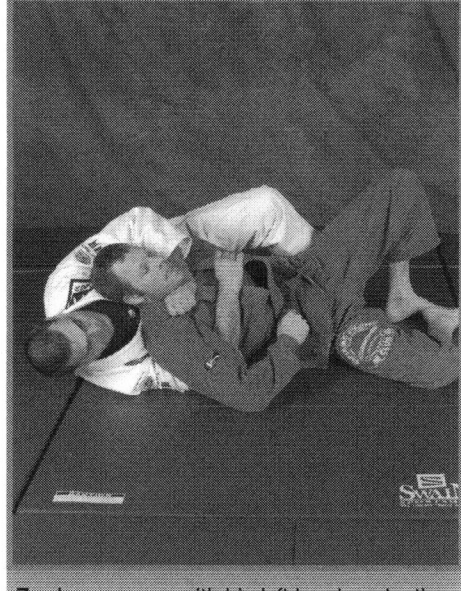

7. he squeezes with his left hand, grabs the other side of the jacket with his right hand...

8. ...and, by pulling down with his right hand and back with his left, applies a devastating finishing choke from the rear.

GROUND CHOKES
FROM THE SIDE

1. Renato is controlling his opponent from a half-side mount position.

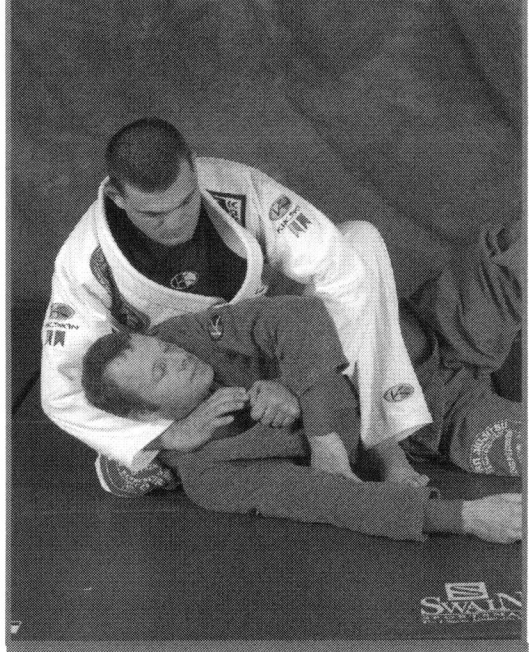

2. He passes his left arm under the opponent's left armpit as he simultaneously reaches with his right hand around the right side of the opponent's neck.

TECHNIQUE 17

3. As soon as he manages to apply pressure with his right knee behind the opponent's neck, Renato reaches for the opponent's left leg...

4. ...and lets his body fall back, to apply a painful rear choke.

GROUND CHOKES

FROM THE SIDE

1. Renato is controlling the opponent from a side position.

2. Then, he grabs the back of the opponent's belt with his left hand and the back of the collar with his right.

3. Renato pulls hard to bring his opponent up.

Technique 18

4. Then, he passes his left hand under the opponent's left armpit...

5. ...as he simultaneously reaches for the left side of the collar with his right hand.

6. Once he has proper control of the situation, Renato pulls hard with his right hand and applies a choke from the side.

GROUND CHOKES
FROM THE SIDE

1. Renato is on the top, controlling the actions of his opponent.

2. He brings his left hand and puts it inside the left side of the opponent's collar.

Technique 19

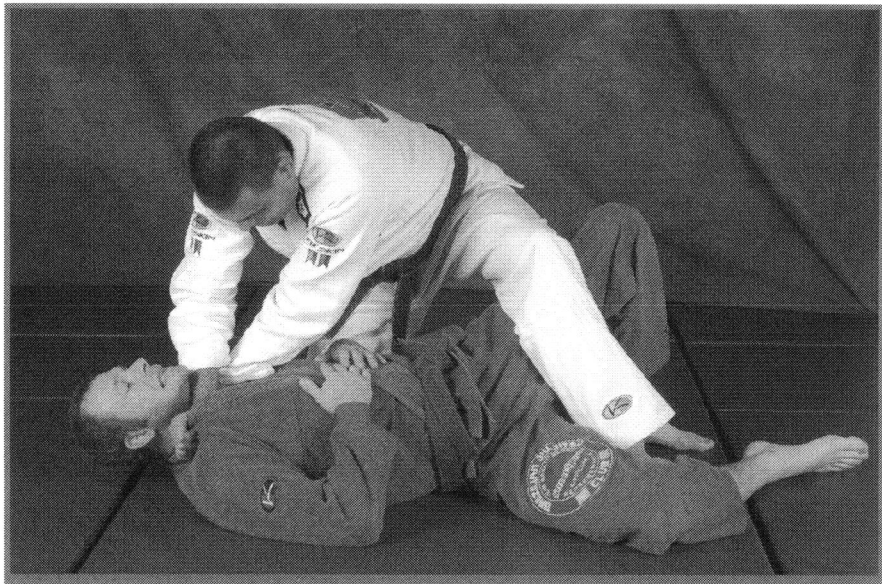

3. Once the left hand is secured deep into the collar, Renato brings the right hand over the left and grabs the outside part of the right side of the gi.

4. He leans forward and applies pressure to execute a frontal choke.

GROUND CHOKES
FROM THE SIDE

1. Renato is on the side, controlling his opponent.

2. He switches the position of the legs...

3. ...to jump and pass the left leg over the opponent's chest...

TECHNIQUE 20

4. ...as he simultaneously pulls hard on the opponent's left arm with his right hand.

5. Then, Renato lifts the arm and passes his left leg under the opponent's head...

6. ...as he positions himself to lock the left foot under the back of his left knee to apply a triangle choke from the mount position.

GROUND CHOKES

GROUND CHOKES
FROM THE SIDE

1. Renato controls his opponent from a knee-on-stomach position.

2. With his right hand, Renato grabs and pulls the opponent's left arm.

3. Then, he creates space to pass his left leg over...

4. ...and secures it under the opponent's neck.

TECHNIQUE 21

5. By pulling the opponent's left arm across his left leg, Renato creates a triangle submission.

6. The opponent makes him roll over the side...

7. ...from where Renato manages to maintain the same tight position...

8. ...to hook his left foot under the back of the right knee to apply a finishing choke, using the triangle.

GROUND CHOKES

GROUND CHOKES

FROM THE SIDE

1. Renato is on the left side of the opponent's body.

2. He moves his left arm and brings it close to the right side of the opponent's head and...

3. ...switches his base by moving the legs so he can get a side control with the arm behind the head of the opponent for better support.

TECHNIQUE 22

4. With his left hand, he reaches to grab the cuff of the right sleeve.

5. Then, he moves his right forearm in front of the opponent's neck and ...

6. leans forward to apply pressure and execute a frontal choke named *Ezequiel*.

GROUND CHOKES
FROM THE SIDE

1. Renato is seated on the left side of the opponent's body.

2. He moves his left arm and brings it close to the right side of the opponent's head.

3. Then, he switches his base by moving the legs so he can get a side control with the arm behind the head of the opponent for better support.

4. With his left hand, he reaches to grab the cuff of the right sleeve.

Technique 23

5. Then, he moves his right forearm in front of the opponent's neck...

6. ...but this time the opponent moves to the side to prevent the choke, so Renato has to adapt by bringing his left knee onto the opponent's stomach...

7. ...to pass over his chest and mount him for full control..

8. From the mount position, he applies a frontal choke.

GROUND CHOKES
FROM THE SIDE

1. Renato approaches the opponent.

2. He brings his left arm under the opponent's left armpit…

Technique 24

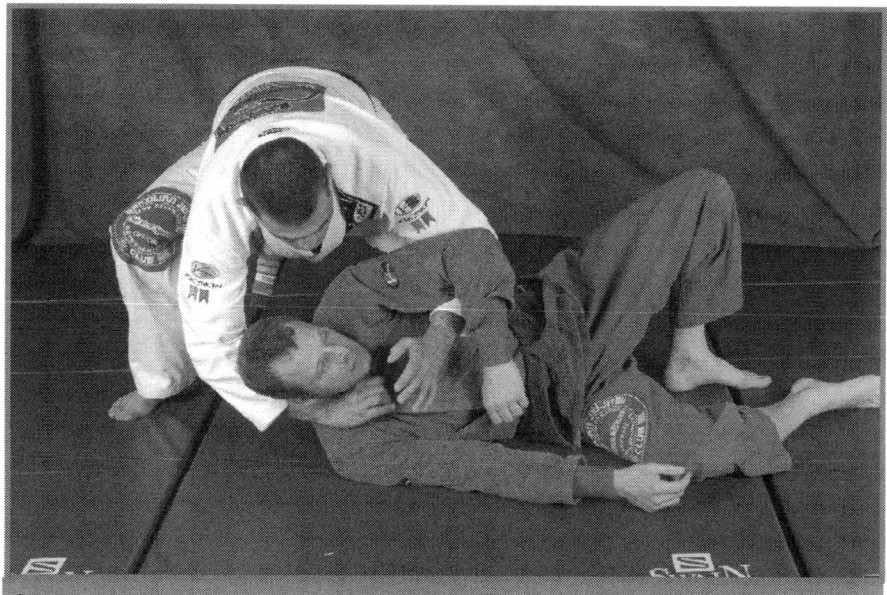

3. ...as he secures the grip on the left side of the collar with his right hand.

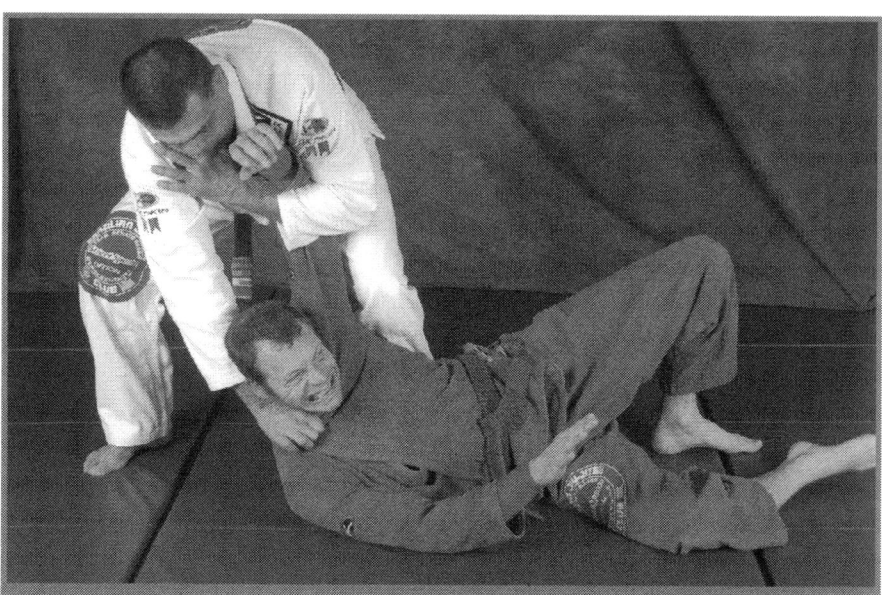

4. By pulling hard with his right hand as he simultaneously controls the left arm of the opponent, Renato applies a finishing choke from the side.

GROUND CHOKES
FROM THE SIDE

1. Renato, standing, is watching his opponent on the ground.

2. Then, he takes a step and brings his left foot to the other side of the opponent's body.

3. Renato begins to move his right knee close to the opponent as he simultaneously grabs the opponent's pants with his left hand.

TECHNIQUE 25

4. With his right hand, he reaches for the right side of the collar.

5. Then, Renato sits down and, by keeping tight grips in all controlling points of the technique, he applies a devastating choke.

GROUND CHOKES
FROM THE GUARD

1. Renato has the opponent inside the closed guard.

2. Now, he moves his right hand and grabs the inside of the right side of the opponent's collar.

3. By turning the hips to the side, he begins to attack for an armlock...

4. ...but the opponent turns slightly and nullifies the attempt.

TECHNIQUE 1

5. Renato then releases the pressure of his legs and...

6. ...secures a tighter grip with his right hand.

7. He lets the opponent's left arm pass to the side...

8. ...which gives him better leverage to put pressure with his legs and go for the one-hand choke.

GROUND CHOKES
FROM THE GUARD

1. Renato has the opponent inside his closed guard.

2. He grabs the opponent's right sleeve and pulls the arm across his body to the right side.

3. Then, he reaches around the opponent's neck with his left hand...

TECHNIQUE 2

4. ...and grabs the right side of the collar.

5. With full control of the opponent, Renato leans backwards and applies a side choke.

GROUND CHOKES

FROM THE GUARD

1. The opponent is inside Renato's closed guard.

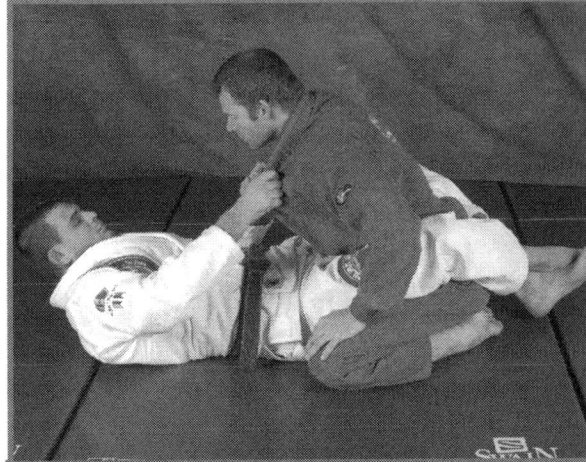

2. Renato grabs with both hands the collar of the opponent's gi.

3. He pulls hard to open space...

TECHNIQUE 3

4. ...so he can, without releasing the grip of his right hand, wrap the collar around the neck of the opponent.

5. Then, he tightens it up by bringing the right elbow close to his body...

6. ...and applies a finishing choke as he simultaneously pulls with his hand and pushes away with the legs.

GROUND CHOKES
FROM THE GUARD

1. Renato has the opponent inside his closed guard.

2. The opponent initiates the attack by grabbing both of Renato's lapels.

TECHNIQUE 4

3. Renato pushes one hand away...

4. ...and brings his left leg up to the level of the opponent's shoulder.

5. Then, he pulls the opponent's left arm across his body...

(CONTINUED ON NEXT PAGE)

GROUND CHOKES

FROM THE GUARD
(CONTINUED FROM PREVIOUS PAGE)

6. ...and, with his right hand, reaches the opponent's head and pulls it down.

7. Simultaneously, he pulls the other arm to the left side.

Technique 4

8. Securing the left arm with his left hand, Renato now grabs his own left ankle...

9. ...and brings it under the back of his right knee to apply a triangle choke.

GROUND CHOKES
FROM THE GUARD

1. Renato has his opponent inside the open guard.

2. He brings both legs back between the opponent's arms...

3. ...and pulls his left leg to the outside so he can place it over the opponent's right shoulder.

4. Then, Renato brings the opponent's body closer by pulling from both sleeves.

Technique 5

5. Once the opponent's body is closer, Renato grabs the left arm and puts it across his stomach...

6. ...and immediately secures the tight position by grabbing his left ankle with the right hand.

7. Once he has locked that position firmly...

8. ...he grabs the opponent's head and pulls it down to apply a triangle choke.

GROUND CHOKES
FROM THE GUARD

1. The opponent is inside Renato's closed guard.

2. Renato moves his hips and tries to attack with an armlock.

3. The opponent feels it and reacts by pulling his right arm out.

TECHNIQUE 6

4. Renato has to adjust; he immediately moves his hips to the other direction and brings his left leg over the opponent's head as he simultaneously pulls his left arm across the body.

5. Then, he secures the position by putting his left ankle under the back of his right knee to apply a triangle choke.

GROUND CHOKES
FROM THE BACK

1. The opponent is on all fours and Renato is on his right side trying to control him.

2. Renato passes his left hand under the opponent's left arm...

3. ...to grab and secure the opponent's hand.

TECHNIQUE 1

4. Then, he reaches for the left side of the collar...

5. ...and, by pulling back, he chokes the opponent out.

GROUND CHOKES
FROM THE BACK

1. Renato is ready to attack the opponent from the side.

2. He moves his right hand and grabs the left side of the opponent's collar as he simultaneously controls the body by placing his left hand on the lower back.

TECHNIQUE 2

3. Renato then reaches the opponent's left ankle...

4. ...and, by simultaneously pulling back with the left and right hands, he applies pressure to execute a side choke.

GROUND CHOKES
FROM THE BACK

1. Renato is behind the opponent.

2. He begins his attack by leaning forward...

3. ...to pass both arms under the opponent's armpits...

4. ...so he can reach and grab both sides of the collar.

TECHNIQUE 3

5. Without releasing the grips, Renato moves his left leg to the outside…

6. …and establishes his base so he can let the left hand go…

7. …to bring it behind the opponent's neck…

8. …in order to apply a finishing choke.

GROUND CHOKES
FROM THE BACK

1. Renato is behind the opponent.

2. With his left hand he reaches to grab the back of the opponent's collar.

3. Then, he pulls him back, bringing his body up.

TECHNIQUE 4

4. Now, Renato passes his left arm around the opponent's neck...

5. ...puts his right hand behind the head...

6. ...and squeezes tightly to apply a rear choke.

GROUND CHOKES
FROM THE BACK

1. Renato is controlling the opponent from the back.

2. With his left hand, he reaches to pass his left arm around the opponent's neck...

3. ...as he simultaneously brings his right hand across...

Technique 5

4. ...to set the hands in position for...

5. a rear choke. Remember to maintain control at all times of the opponent's body by applying pressure with the legs. Never cross your feet.

GROUND CHOKES
FROM THE BACK

1. Renato is controlling the opponent from the back.

2. He reaches out under the arms and grabs both sides of the opponent's collar to be able to pull down the jacket.

3. Then, Renato brings his left hand across and in front of the opponent's neck and grabs the left side of the collar.

TECHNIQUE 6

4. With his right hand, he grabs the other side of the jacket...

5. ...and, by pulling down with his right hand and across with left, Renato applies a rear choke.

GROUND CHOKES

FROM THE BACK

1. Renato is controlling the opponent from the back.

2. He reaches with his left hand and brings it in front of the opponent's neck to grab the right side of the collar.

TECHNIQUE 7

3. Then, he starts moving his body to the right side as he simultaneously controls the opponent's right arm with his right hand.

4. Renato leans back to the ground and, while controlling the opponent's left arm with his leg and the right with his right hand, he applies a finishing choke from the rear.

GROUND CHOKES

FROM THE BACK

1. Renato, controlling the opponent from the back, reaches with his left hand and brings it in front of the opponent's neck to grab the right side of the collar as he secures the opponent's right leg with his right hand.

2. Now, he brings his left leg over and puts it on top of the opponent's left arm...

TECHNIQUE 8

3. ...as he simultaneously leans back, letting his body fall onto the ground to apply a one-hand choke from behind.

GROUND CHOKES

FROM THE BACK

1. Renato is controlling the opponent from the back.

2. He passes his left hand around the opponent's neck...

3. ...in a counterclockwise motion...

TECHNIQUE 9

4. ...that allows him to bring the opponent off balance...

5. ...as he secures the grip with his right hand...

6. ...to apply a painful reverse rear choke from behind.

GROUND CHOKES

FROM THE BACK

1. Renato is taking the opponent's back.

2. He brings his left hand across the front of the opponent's neck...

3. ...and also brings his left foot over the opponent's left shoulder.

4. The opponent, feeling the attack attempt, leans forward to avoid it.

TECHNIQUE 10

5. Renato then moves his hips to the side and hooks his left ankle under the back of his right knee.

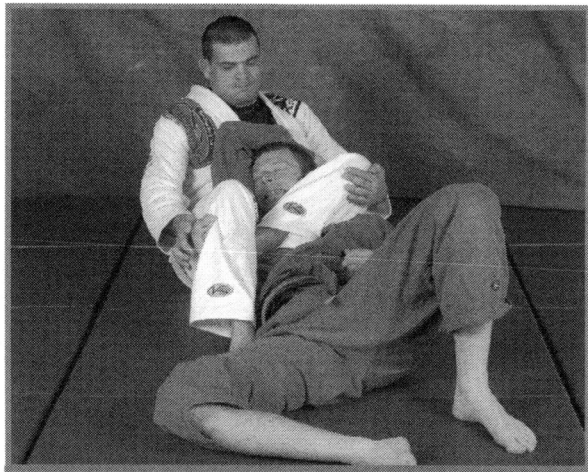

6. He secures a tight position by pushing his left knee inside…

7. …and applies a rear triangle choke.

GROUND CHOKES

FROM THE BACK

1. Renato is taking the opponent's back.

2. He brings his left hand across the front of the opponent's neck…

3. …to prepare a rear choke…

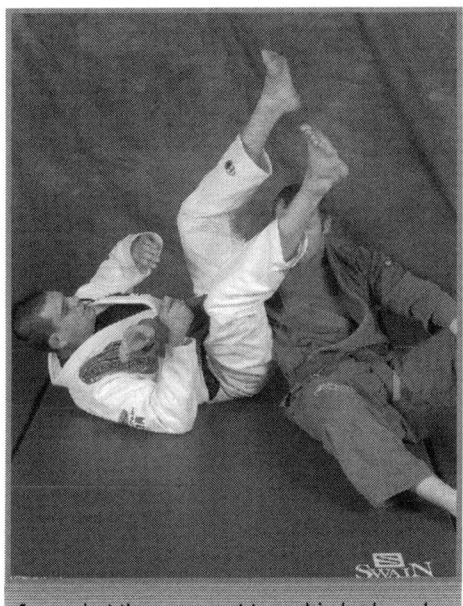

4. …but the opponent turns his body and Renato falls to the side.

TECHNIQUE 11

5. The opponent tries to turn around, but Renato controls his action...

6. ...and hooks his right leg over the opponent's left shoulder...

7. ...as he simultaneously secures the right ankle under the back of the left knee to apply a triangle choke.

GROUND CHOKES
FROM THE MOUNT

1. Renato controls his opponent from the mount position.

2. He begins to move his left arm...

3. ...and brings it under the opponent's neck.

4. Then, he reaches and grabs the cuff of the right sleeve of his own gi.

Technique 1

5. Now, Renato brings his right hand in front of the opponent's neck…

6. …leans forward to apply pressure and…

7. …submits his opponent using an Ezequiel choke.

GROUND CHOKES

FROM THE MOUNT

1. Renato is controlling his opponent from the mount position.

2. The opponent begins to roll to the side and Renato allows him to do so.

3. Then, he brings his left foot close and stops the action, adopting a side mount position.

4. From here, Renato reaches out with his left hand and passes it under the opponent's left arm.

Technique 2

5. Now, he grabs the left side of the collar with his right hand...

6. ...as he simultaneously uses his left hand to pull up the opponent's left arm...

7. ...so he can apply a choke from the side mount position.

GROUND CHOKES

FROM THE MOUNT

1. Renato is seated on top of the opponent on a mount position.

2. He passes his left leg over the opponent's right shoulder...

3. ...and lifts the opponent's head with his right hand.

TECHNIQUE 3

4. With his left hand, Renato pulls the opponent's left arm across…

5. …to create space to grab his head with both hands…

6. …so he can try to apply a triangle choke from the top.

(CONTINUED ON NEXT PAGE)

GROUND CHOKES

FROM THE MOUNT
(CONTINUED FROM PREVIOUS PAGE)

7. The opponent feels the submission attempt and starts rolling to the side to unbalance Renato...

8. ...who lets the counter move take place...

9. ...but without losing control of the opponent by holding his head close to his chest.

Technique 3

10. Renato now pulls the opponent's arm across his body…

11. …secures his left ankle under the back of his right knee…

12. …and applies a triangle choke.

GROUND CHOKES
FACING THE GUARD

1. Renato is inside the opponent's closed guard.

2. The opponent's pulls Renato closer by using his legs.

3. Renato takes advantage of that and brings his left arm under the back of the opponent's neck.

Technique 1

4. Then, he reaches for the cuff of his right sleeve and grabs it with his left hand.

5. Renato brings his right forearm in front of the opponent's neck...

6. ...and applies a finishing choke from inside the guard.

GROUND CHOKES

FACING THE GUARD

1. Renato is inside the opponent's closed guard.

2. The opponent tries to unbalance Renato by using his legs…

TECHNIQUE 2

3. ...but Renato reacts by using his opponent's energy to reach and grab the top of the opponent's front collar with his left hand...

4. ...as he simultaneously pulls on the other side of the jacket with his right hand, applying a front choke from inside the guard.

GROUND CHOKES

FACING THE GUARD

1. The opponent is controlling Renato's positions inside the guard.

2. When the opponent pulls back hard, Renato lets his body go and positions himself with his left arm next to the left side of the opponent's head.

3. Then, he wraps his arm around and behind the opponent's neck...

TECHNIQUE 3

4. ...until he can reach and grab the left side of the opponent's collar.

5. Once he has secured the grip with his left hand...

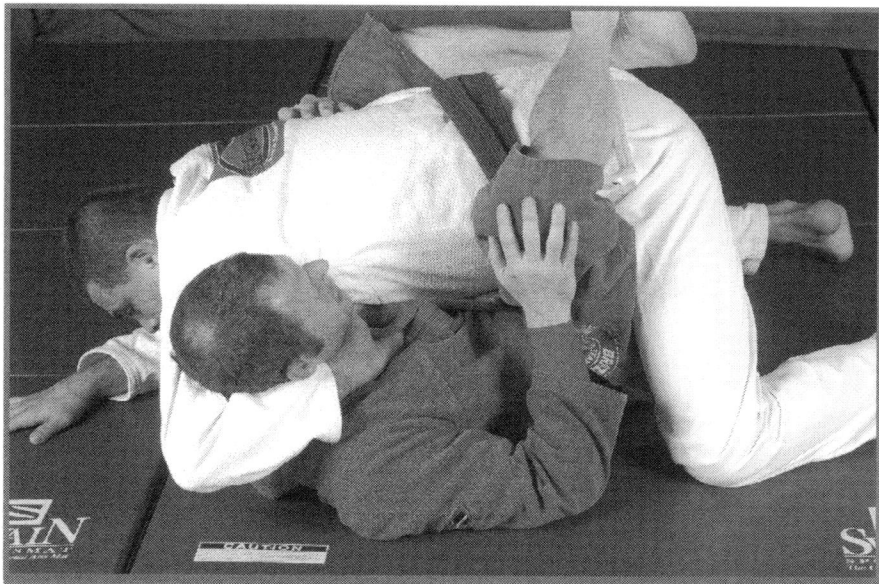

6. ...Renato leans forward and applies pressure to finish the opponent off with a reverse one-hand choke from inside the guard

GROUND CHOKES

FACING THE GUARD

1. Renato is inside the opponent's open guard.

2. He tries to bring his left arm across and around the opponent's right leg...

TECHNIQUE 4

3. ...in order to grab the opposite side of the opponent's collar...

4. ...in an attempt to pass the opponent's guard.

(CONTINUED ON NEXT PAGE)

GROUND CHOKES
FACING THE GUARD
(CONTINUED FROM PREVIOUS PAGE)

5. The opponent readjusts his position and prevents Renato from passing the guard…

6. …by controlling his upper body with the right hand…

7. …and by flexing his legs backwards.

TECHNIQUE 4

8. Renato, feeling the impossibility of passing the guard, changes his strategy and leans forward with all his body weigh to apply a frontal choke by using his left forearm across the opponent's neck.

9. SIDE VIEW.

GROUND CHOKES

CONCLUSION

CONCLUSION

Now that you have finished this book, what have you learned? Hopefully, nothing less than a series of practical and efficient techniques to become a successful Brazilian Jiu Jitsu practitioner. These techniques will help you to succeed in competition and self-defense, but simply reading through these pages is not enough. You must consistently practice each technique with a training partner, exploring all the possibilities of each movement, until you obtain the desired results based on your body style, athletic ability, and physical attributes.

Not all these techniques will work for every Jiu Jitsu practitioner. Once you have a basic framework in place, you must fine-tune each technique until it fits your game. The enjoyable part of the art of Brazilian Jiu Jitsu is that everyone can adapt and personalize it. While the basics are the same, the application of the basics is as different and varied as each practitioner. When practiced under the guidance of an instructor, or with the assistance of a willing training partner, the techniques, principles, and methods explained in this book will be effective, because they have been tested and proven in the laboratory of practical experience and the crucible of real competition.

Your task now is simple: go out and have fun with them.

The Publishers

NOTES

Printed in Great Britain
by Amazon